POPULAR
ANTIQUES
and their
VALUES

Compiled and Edited by

TONY CURTIS

While every care has been taken in the compiling of information contained in this volume the publishers cannot accept any liability for loss, financial or otherwise, incurred by reliance placed on the information herein.

1st Edition October 1971
2nd Impression November 1971
3rd Impression December 1971
4th Impression January 1972
5th Impression March 1972
6th Impression May 1972
7th Impression June 1972
8th Impression August 1972

2nd Edition August 1973 (Revised Prices)
2nd Impression December 1973
3rd Impression June 1974
4th Impression December 1974

3rd Edition June 1975 (Revised Prices)
2nd Impression October 1975
3rd Impression April 1976
4th Impression August 1976

4th Edition April 1977 (Revised Prices)

LYLE PUBLICATIONS LIMITED

GLENMAYNE   GALASHIELS   SELKIRKSHIRE   SCOTLAND

CONTENTS

Printed in Great Britain by

APOLLO PRESS   DOMINION WAY   WORTHING   SUSSEX

INTRODUCTION

With the increase in popularity of Antiques and Antique Collecting a need has arisen for a comprehensive reference work of detailed illustrations and prices to be used as a guide to current market values.

The purpose of this publication is to make it easy for those either buying, selling, or merely interested in the value of the pieces in their own home, to identify and have a knowledge of the price an Antique Dealer is likely to pay for a piece in average condition.

The illustrations have been most carefully chosen to bring your attention to the significance of detail, which could appear to be an unimportant variation in style but may represent not only fifty years in age but fifty pounds in value. This being only one important factor to be taken into consideration when making an estimate of an average piece.

The condition of an Antique is of great importance. Most collectors and dealers will agree that it is the exception rather than the rule to find a piece of furniture that has not sustained damage or been altered in accordance with fashion at some time during its life. A tall piece may have had feet cut down, or a naturally light wood stained a darker shade and thereby spoiled. When a set of handles have been changed the original set are likely to be irreplaceable. A small piece of veneer missing may seem of little consequence but it will take the work of a craftsman to put it right which costs both time and money.

When making any calculations it is wise to remember that the dealer may have to spend as much having the piece put in a saleable condition as he has originally paid for that same item. One must also allow for his profit margin. At all times the cost of restoration must be taken into account, for even the most rare piece, if damaged is imperfect, and therefore of lesser value than the perfect example.

The current value of an Antique varies enormously in different areas. What is fashionable in one county may be totally disregarded in another which accounts for the amount of trading between dealers who come from different parts of the country. This will also happen when one dealer is more knowledgeable than another or a specialist in a particular field. One dealer may find it more profitable to turn his stock over frequently in order to keep his money 'working' for him and will therefore buy and sell while showing a very modest profit.

Another may treat his stock as an investment and can afford to wait for a higher price. Once a trend has been established in a particular period or style, the value will remain high for as long as that trend lasts. This can happen in a locality where overseas buyers make regular calls buying 'their' goods at 'their' price until they have completed a shipment, when the price will be revised in accordance with demand, and will probably return to normal.

With well over 1,300 illustrations we cover both the expensive collectors items and those, which although not in the true sense Antiques, are still much sought after in the Antique Trade, along with a price guide which having taken all relevant factors into account, is to the best of our knowledge a fair estimate of the price a dealer will pay for a piece in average condition. This will not be his selling price as has been explained.

We have had a great deal of help from private collectors and dealers during our research into this volume and wish to express our thanks to all concerned.

We wish you a smooth path in this exciting field.

TONY CURTIS

MONARCHS

HENRY 1V	1399 - 1413
HENRY V	1413 - 1422
HENRY V1	1422 - 1461
EDWARD 1V	1461 - 1483
EDWARD V	1483 - 1483
RICHARD 111	1483 - 1485
HENRY V11	1485 - 1509
HENRY V111	1509 - 1547
EDWARD V1	1547 - 1553
MARY	1553 - 1558
ELIZABETH	1558 - 1603
JAMES 1	1603 - 1625
CHARLES 1	1625 - 1649
COMMONWEALTH	1649 - 1660
CHARLES 11	1660 - 1685
JAMES 11	1685 - 1689
WILLIAM & MARY	1689 - 1695
WILLIAM 111	1695 - 1702
ANNE	1702 - 1714
GEORGE 1	1714 - 1727
GEORGE 11	1727 - 1760
GEORGE 111	1760 - 1820
GEORGE 1V	1820 - 1830
WILLIAM 1V	1830 - 1837
VICTORIA	1837 - 1901
EDWARD V11	1901 - 1910

PERIODS

TUDOR PERIOD	1485 - 1603
ELIZABETHAN PERIOD	1558 - 1603
INIGO JONES	1572 - 1652
JACOBEAN PERIOD	1603 - 1688
STUART PERIOD	1603 - 1714
A. C. BOULLE	1642 - 1732
LOUIS XIV PERIOD	1643 - 1715
GRINLING GIBBONS	1648 - 1726
CROMWELLIAN PERIOD	1649 - 1660
CAROLEAN PERIOD	1660 - 1685
WILLIAM KENT	1684 - 1748
WILLIAM & MARY PERIOD	1689 - 1702
QUEEN ANNE PERIOD	1702 - 1714
GEORGIAN PERIOD	1714 - 1820
T. CHIPPENDALE	1715 - 1762
LOUIS XV PERIOD	1723 - 1774
A. HEPPLEWHITE	1727 - 1788
ADAM PERIOD	1728 - 1792
ANGELICA KAUFMANN	1741 - 1807
T. SHERATON	1751 - 1806
LOUIS XVI	1774 - 1793
T. SHEARER	(circa) 1780
REGENCY PERIOD	1800 - 1830
EMPIRE PERIOD	1804 - 1815
VICTORIAN PERIOD	1830 - 1901
EDWARDIAN PERIOD	1901 - 1910

Victorian oak framed
wall barometer. **£10**

Late Victorian baro-
meter in a carved oak
case. **£25**

Sheraton
period wheel
barometer.
£85

Victorian walnut
framed barometer with
moulded edge. **£35**

An early Victorian
rosewood cased banjo
barometer inlaid with
mother of pearl. **£80**

Victorian mahogany
tulip top barometer.
£40

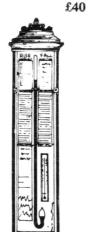

Sheraton mahogany
cased barometer with
mirror and boxwood
string inlay. **£100**

Georgian mahogany
cased barometer with
hygrometer, thermom-
eter and clock. **£240**

Georgian walnut cased
cistern pediment
barometer. **£190**

A Victorian Admiral
Fitzroy barometer in
an oak case. **£55**

Late Georgian mah-
ogany stick barometer.
£165

19th century Dutch
marquetry bed 3ft,
wide. **£300**

19th century red lacquer
and gilt bed 4ft. wide,
decorated with domestic
scenes. **£250**

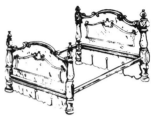

Late Victorian figured
mahogany bed, 4ft. 6ins.
wide. **£35**

Italian carved walnut
four poster bed. **£425**

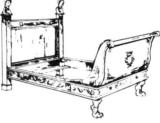

Regency mahogany bed
with ormolu decoration
and paw feet. **£310**

Victorian brass bed 3ft
wide. **£70**

17th century oak four
poster bed. **£475**

A Victorian brass half
tester bed 4ft. 6ins.
wide. **£160**

Early Georgian mahogany
tester with original drapes
4ft. 6ins. wide. **£450**

Early 19th century oak cot. **£65**

Victorian wicker work cradle. **£15**

Late Georgian suspended cot in canework on a mahogany stand. **£95**

Hepplewhite mahogany canework crib. **£135**

Sheraton period crib with a mechanical rocker. **£200**

17th century oak cradle **£110**

19th century country made chair back crib in elm. **£60**

A Victorian brass crib. **£65**

Late 17th century oak hooded cradle. **£95**

BOOKCASES

Victorian mahogany standing bookcase. **£45**

Edwardian mahogany revolving bookcase inlaid with bone and ivory. **£85**

Victorian mahogany hanging shelves with small drawer in the base. **£45**

Georgian mahogany bookcase with fluted columns. **£400**

Victorian mahogany open bookshelves. **£70**

Regency brass inlaid rosewood bookcase. **£440**

Late Georgian mahogany breakfront bookcase with astragal glazed doors and cupboards to base. **£1,750**

Chippendale mahogany bookcase with carved cornice and cluster column pilasters. **£450**

Victorian breakfront bookcase in mahogany with glazed doors enclosing adjustable shelves. **£700**

14

Regency period open
shelf brass inlaid book-
case in rosewood with
marble top.   **£310**

Late Georgian satinwood
bookcase having centre
shelves flanked by cup-
boards.   **£300**

Small Regency mahogany
bookcase on stand with a
brass grille door.   **£385**

Georgian standing book-
shelves in finely grained
mahogany.   **£375**

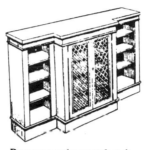

Regency mahogany break-
front bookcase with brass
grille to cupboard doors.
£315

Regency period ebonised
standing bookshelves
having brass stringing and
painted panels to cupboards
and back.   **£340**

George III mahogany breakfront bookcase with satinwood stringing having
adjustable shelves enclosed
by astragal glazed doors.
£8,000

Regency period Gothic style
bookcase with glazed doors
and cupboards enclosing
drawers to base.   **£325**

Georgian mahogany break-
front bookcase with glazed
doors to upper section
and cupboards below. **£1,800**

BUREAUX

18th century oak bureau with fluted pillars. **£260**

Edwardian inlaid cylinder front bureau. **£225**

Victorian carved oak bureau. **£145**

Late 19th century lacquered bureau on bracket feet. **£130**

Sheraton style sandalwood bureau. **£380**

Early 18th century oak bureau with stand. **£200**

Edwardian mahogany bureau with shell inlay and bracket feet. **£120**

Early Georgian mahogany bureau on stand. **£550**

Edwardian oak bureau on stretcher base. **£30**

19th century French mahogany bureau with inlaid flowers and ormolu mounts. **£700**

Dutch marquetry bonheur-de-jour. **£800**

Edwardian Sheraton style bureau with cylinder top and cupboard under. **£165**

Dutch mahogany bombe front, cylinder desk with shaped interior. **£900**

French marquetry and rosewood bureau with brass gallery and cabriole legs. **£300**

Edwardian inlaid mahogany cylinder front bureau. **£185**

Early 18th century oak bureau. **£525**

William and Mary walnut veneered bureau. **£2,850**

Georgian mahogany bureau on splayed feet. **£250**

Queen Anne bureau in walnut with herringbone banding. **£1,250**

Queen Anne walnut bureau or stand. **£3,250**

Edwardian inlaid mahogany bureau with cupboard under. **£110**

Small George III mahogany bureau on ogee feet. **£425**

William and Mary walnut bureau on stand. **£1,600**

Small William and Mary oak bureau with shaped interior. **£400**

BUREAU BOOKCASES

George II style red
and gold lacquered
bureau bookcase.
£2,000

Georgian mahogany
bureau bookcase with
astragal glazed doors.
£800

Small 18th century
Dutch marquetry
bureau cabinet.
£3,000

Victorian mahogany
cylinder front bureau
bookcase. **£185**

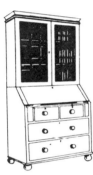

Edwardian oak bureau
bookcase with leaded
glazing. **£90**

Edwardian inlaid mahog-
any bureau bookcase.
£280

Small Queen Anne
walnut bureau book-
case. **£6,500**

Early 20th century
oak bureau bookcase.
£60

George II mahogany
bureau cabinet on
ogee feet. **£2,000**

Hepplewhite period
bureau bookcase in
mahogany with latti-
ced glazed doors.
£2,750

17th century walnut
bureau bookcase with
Vauxhall mirror doors.
£3,250

Early 18th century
Flemish marquetry
bureau cabinet **£3,250**

18

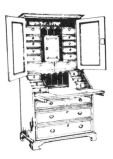

Mid 18th century bureau bookcase in mahogany. **£1,250**

Early 18th century walnut bureau bookcase with panelled doors. **£2,600**

Queen Anne walnut bureau bookcase with a stepped interior **£1,900**

Late 18th century mahogany bureau bookcase with glazed doors in the Gothic manner. **£850**

Small Queen Anne bureau bookcase with the upper front having a moulded cornice and a bevelled mirror door. **£7,000**

Queen Anne walnut bureau bookcase with original mirrors and brasses. **£2,850**

George II walnut bureau bookcase with double domed top. **£2,100**

Edwardian walnut bureau bookcase on cabriole leg supports. **£140**

Burr yew wood cylinder desk and bookcase with satinwood, kingwood and tulipwood enrichments. **£8,500**

Small George II red walnut bureau bookcase with original bevelled Vauxhall mirror door flanked by fluted pilasters. **£3,250**

George I yew wood bureau bookcase with broken arched pediment. **£3,500**

Edwardian Sheraton style cylinder front bureau bookcase with glazed doors. **£450**

CABINETS

Edwardian inlaid mahogany music cabinet of six drawers, 3ft.1in. high. **£50**

German cabinet profusely inlaid with town scenes, musical trophies and flowers, 20½in. wide, circa 1600. **£820**

Georgian mahogany collector's cabinet, 63cm. wide. **£170**

Oak cabinet by Charles Rennie Mackintosh, circa 1905. **£1,500**

19th century ebonised and red boulle two-door side cabinet with ormolu mounts and marble top. **£595**

19th century kingwood and ormolu mounted side cabinet. **£295**

William and Mary cabinet with original stand, circa 1690. **£800**

Late 18th century cabinet on stand with Chinese decoration. **£400**

Small Chinese Chippendale style cabinet. **£260**

Small Victorian burr
walnut canterbury. **£110**

Late Victorian ebonised
canterbury with gilt
decoration. **£60**

Regency mahogany
canterbury on fine
turned legs. **£145**

Regency mahogany
canterbury with
drawer. **£140**

Regency mahogany
canterbury on short
turned legs with brass
castors. **£150**

Victorian rosewood
canterbury with drawer
to base. **£110**

Georgian mahogany
canterbury on fine
turned feet terminating
in brass castors. **£145**

Victorian burr walnut
music canterbury with
fretted supports and
drawer to base. **£140**

Unusual Georgian mahogany
canterbury with drawer to
base. **£165**

21

CHARS

Late Victorian oak framed dining chair.
Set of 4 - **£55**
Set of 6 - **£85**

Early Victorian simulated rosewood bedroom chair with cane seat.
Set of 4 - **£70**
Set of 6 - **£110**

Late 19th century dining chair with brass ornamentation.
Set of 4 - **£90**
Set of 6 - **£150**

19th century elm kitchen chair.
Set of 4 - **£30**
Set of 6 - **£50**

19th century Windsor wheelback chair in beech.
Set of 4 - **£40**
Set of 6 - **£70**

Victorian cabriole leg dining chair in rosewood.
Set of 4 - **£165**
Set of 6 - **£360**

Early Victorian mahogany balloon back dining chair.
Set of 4 - **£80**
Set of 6 - **£150**

Victorian cabriole leg dining chair in walnut.
Set of 4 - **£155**
Set of 6 - **£325**

William IV mahogany frame dining chair upholstered in leather.
Set of 4 - **£100**
Set of 6 - **£180**

Hepplewhite period mahogany dining chair.
Set of 4 - **£200**
Set of 6 - **£425**

French rococo style dining chair in gilt-wood.
Set of 4 - **£180**
Set of 6 - **£350**

Hepplewhite period dining chair in mahogany.
Set of 4 - **£200**
Set of 6 - **£425**

Victorian mahogany bar back chair on turned legs.
Set of 4 - **£90**
Set of 6 - **£160**

Chippendale Gothic style mahogany chair on square legs with stretchers.
Set of 4 - **£425**
Set of 6 - **£900**

Mid 18th century mahogany servants hall chair.
Single - **£45**
Pair - **£110**

Victorian splat back kitchen chair in elm.
Set of 4 - **£40**
Set of 6 - **£80**

19th century Chippendale style mahogany chair with ball and claw feet.
Set of 4 - **£185**
Set of 6 - **£325**

Derbyshire oak dining chair.
Single - **£60**
Pair - **£140**

Early 19th century mahogany dining chair on turned legs.
Set of 4 - **£155**
Set of 6 - **£300**

Regency mahogany dining chair with 'X' frame back.
Set of 4 - **£185**
Set of 6 - **£365**

Regency mahogany dining chair with cane seat and back and sabre legs.
Set of 4 - **£200**
Set of 6 - **£425**

Charles II walnut dining chair.
Single - **£120**
Pair - **£260**

Regency period mahogany dining chair with scimitar shaped legs.
Set of 4 - **£160**
Set of 6 - **£350**

Regency rope back dining chair in rosewood with sabre legs.
Set of 4 - **£240**
Set of 6 - **£525**

CHAIRS

Late Georgian Windsor
wheel back armchair
in yew wood.   **£95**

Regency mahogany
childs chair and
stand.   **£120**

Ebonised wood, rush
seated Shetland chair.
    £40

Windsor wheelback
childs high chair in
elm.   **£45**

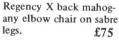

Hepplewhite period mahog-
any elbow chair on fine
tapered legs.   **£85**

Regency X back mahog-
any elbow chair on sabre
legs.   **£75**

Hepplewhite shield
and feathers back
elbow chair in
mahogany.   **£90**

Edwardian inlaid
mahogany elbow
chair on square
tapering legs with
spade feet.   **£30**

William IV mahogany
elbow chair on turned
legs.   **£45**

Fine Hepplewhite
period armchair on
tapering legs with
stretchers.   **£130**

William IV dining chair
upholstered in brown
hide.   **£45**

Regency period
ebonised elbow
chair with splayed
legs.   **£80**

24

Victorian smokers chair in elm. **£20**

Charles II walnut high chair. **£750**

Yorkshire ladder back armchair in elm and oak. **£35**

Jacobean oak hall chair carved with scrolls and conventional floral ornament. **£200**

Hepplewhite style mahogany wheel back elbow chair. **£55**

Edwardian inlaid mahogany corner chair. **£35**

Hepplewhite mahogany spindle back elbow chair. **£85**

Sheraton period painted armchair. **£145**

Victorian papier mache salon chair. **£125**

18th century padouk wood armchair. **£200**

George I walnut veneered armchair. on carved cabriole legs with ball and claw feet. **£600**

Queen Anne black japanned chair with caned seat and back. **£750**

CHAIRS

Edwardian ebonised
horseshoe back chair.
£25

Victorian nursing chair
upholstered in original
bead and needlework cover.
£65 **£115**

Victorian walnut Preiu Dieu
chair on cabriole leg
supports. **£65**

Edwardian inlaid walnut
nursing chair. **£60**

Victorian Preiu Dieu chair
supported on turned legs.
£25 **£35**

Victorian walnut ladies
chair with original tapestry cover. **£135**

Victorian balloon back
ladies chair on cabriole leg
supports. **£140**

Victorian walnut frame
horseshoe back smokers
chair. **£40**

Victorian iron frame chair
on turned legs. **£60**

Hepplewhite **period** Gainsborough
chair upholstered in green hide.
£550

French Empire giltwood
elbow chair. **£175**

**Georgian Bergere
chair in satinwood.
£180.**

26

Victorian Abbotsford chair in walnut. **£65**

Small Victorian buttoned sewing chair. **£55**

Late Victorian armchair. **£25**

Victorian mahogany cabriole leg grandfather chair. **£160**

Regency library chair with original leather cover. **£190**

Victorian rosewood gents chair. **£120**

French fauteuil in carved giltwood with original tapestry cover. **£180**

Georgian manogany library chair with sliding writing compartment. **£325**

Victorian mahogany block arm grandfather chair on turned legs. **£115**

George II mahogany armchair on cluster column legs. **£600**

Queen Anne winged easy chair. **£650**

Chippendale period mahogany armchair on carved cabriole legs. **£650**

27

Victorian Wellington chest veneered in rosewood. **£140**

Victorian stripped pine chest of drawers on turned feet. **£30**

Dutch oak bombe chest 3ft. wide. **£325**

William and Mary walnut chest 3ft. 2ins. wide. **£600**

William and Mary cabinet with walnut oyster veneer and barley twist legs with cross stretchers. **£1,000**

Period oak chest of drawers on bun feet. **£250**

Dutch marquetry tallboy with frieze drawer. **£450**

18th century mahogany tallboy with brass capitals and carved cornice. **£325**

Georgian mahogany tallboy with Chinese lattice work frieze. **£450**

Small Georgian bow front chest of drawers in well figured mahogany with a flush caddy top and splayed feet, 2ft. 9ins. wide. **£275**

Victorian mahogany chest of drawers with barley twist columns to the front edge. **£30**

Queen Anne bachelors chest in walnut 2ft. 7ins. wide. **£2,250**

George I walnut chest of four long drawers, with brushing slide and wide crossbanding. **£700**

Queen Anne walnut chest on stand with oak lined drawers. **£750**

Sheraton satinwood bow fronted chest, crossbanded in tulipwood with ebony and boxwood stringing, with a brushing slide **£1,300**

Victorian mahogany tallboy on splay feet, with boxwood stringing. **£150**

George I crossbanded walnut tallboy having a Norwich Sunburst decoration 3ft. 7ins. wide. **£860**

18th century walnut tallboy with fluted pilasters to the top section. **£1,000**

CHIFFONIERS & CREDENZAS

Victorian mahogany chiffonier with rococo carving. **£90**

Fine Regency chiffonier in rosewood. **£375**

Victorian mahogany chiffonier with panelled cupboard doors. **£80**

Late Victorian mahogany chiffonier with single drawer and cupboard below. **£35**

Regency cabinet in rosewood with brass inlaid frieze drawer and brass grille to the doors. **£350**

Regency chiffonier in rosewood with paw feet. **£340**

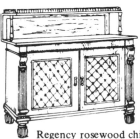

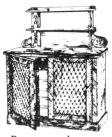

Regency rosewood chiffonier with brass grille to the doors and reeded columns. **£300**

Small Regency brass inlaid chiffonier with brass grille to the door. 2ft.wide. **£325**

Regency mahogany chiffonier with brass grille doors and gallery. **£350**

Regency mahogany buffet with brass string inlay and cupboard doors lined with green silk. **£225**

Victorian mahogany chiffonier with carved mouldings and white marble top. **£110**

Georgian concave side cupboard of finely figured mahogany. **£35**

Regency brass inlaid rosewood chiffonier with panelled doors. **£260**

Early Victorian rosewood chiffonier with panelled cupboard doors. **£100**

Regency mahogany cabinet with mirror panels to cupboard doors. **£250**

Regency brass inlaid chiffonier in rosewood. **£400**

Late Victorian walnut dressing table on cabriole leg front supports. **£45**

Regency chiffonier in figured mahogany **£190**

Regency bookshelves with brass grilles to the doors. **£290**

Victorian burr walnut credenza with centre cupboards flanked by open shelves. **£220**

Regency mahogany chiffonier with a figured marble top. **£275**

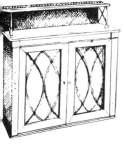

Georgian chiffonier in satinwood. **£440**

Regency mahogany bookcase crossbanded in satinwood. **£325**

Victorian figured mahogany chiffonier **£95**

Staffordshire figure of
Lieutenant Hector
Munro being carried
off by a tiger. **£400**

Royal Dux figure of
a child with dog.
7½ins.high. **£55**

Victorian parian
figure. **£50**

Staffordshire figure of
the young Queen
Victoria. **£90**

Staffordshire figure of
Shakespeare, 18ins. high. **£50**

Leeds creamware
seated Sphinx.
c.1770. **£185**

Victorian parian figure
14ins.,high. **£35**

A 6th century B.C. green
glaze ushabji. **£100**

Capo di Monte group
'The Declaration' by
Guiseppe Gricci. **£12,000**

Victorian Staffordshir
flat back. **£25**

Victorian monkey band
figure. **£28**

19th century Staffordshire
castle. **£30**

Victorian fairing 'The last in
bed to put out the light'. **£2**

Staffordshire group
showing a man being
trampled by a horse.
£600

A T'ang Dynasty horse.
£17,000

Bow porcelain figure of
the infant Bachus and a
leopard. 1750. **£285**

Doulton brown salt glaze
figure of Lord Nelson. **£100**

18th century bust
of Minerva by
Ralph Wood. **£160**

An early Victorian
nodding figure. **£30**

A Mennecy Magot
figure. **£1,000**

19th century Derby
figure. **£95**

Staffordshire flat
back figure. **£24**

Late 18th century Staff-
ordshire pottery figure of
birds. **£250**

Staffordshire cottage
figure. **£155**

18th century Staffordshire
figure of a duck. **£310**

19th century Staffordshire
cottage. **£32**

CHINA

19th century
Prattware vase.
£40

Wedgwood three
colour vase. **£350**

Victorian Goss
china vase. **£1.50**

Small Victorian
yellow ground vase.
£5

Victorian vase 15ins.
high. **£15**

A T'ang Dynasty jar
with a finely cracked
pale greyish glaze.
£1,250

Wedgwood and Bentley
vase and cover. **£1,200**

Small Victorian
Wedgwood vase.
£10

A Doulton Queen
Victoria commemor-
ative jug. **£22**

Victorian shaving mug.
£6

A blue and white Caughley
jug. **£50**

A Dr. Wall Worcester
hot water jug and cover
probably painted in
the atelier of James
Giles. **£1,400**

A blue and brown
Derby plate. **£28**

Sevres porcelain plaque
'La Recreation des
Moissonneurs' forming
the top of a Louis XV
table. **£12,750**

A creamware black
transfer octagonal
plate. **£22**

34

Early 19th century
Worcester teapoy. **£45**

19th century Belleek
jardiniere. **£45**

A Cologne ovoid
vase. **£60**

A Victorian vase with
bird decoration 10 ins
high. **£10**

A 16th century Chinese
Kinrande double gourd
vase. **£30,000**

A Benjamin Lunds vase
7½ ins. high. **£1,000**

Doulton vase
12ins high. **£22**

Minton vase draped with
swans. **£30**

Large Victorian jug. **£14**

Victorian lustre
jug. **£16**

A Ming period white
porcelain ewer
£15,000

Copeland and Garret
jug 1845. **£14**

A Hans Sloane pattern
red anchor Chelsea
plate. **£1,700**

Victorian Staffordshire
plaque. **£20**

19th century green
Wedgwood plate. **£4**

CHINA

A Victorian chamber pot.
£6

Victorian jug and basin set. **£12**

An 18th century Chinese porcelain punch bowl. **£1,500**

19th century Imari bowl. 9ins. diameter. **£14**

A 19th century blue and white foot bath. **£25**

A Sunderland lustre punch bowl. 12ins., diameter. **£40**

Victorian feeding cup. **£3**

Leeds creamware mug. 8ins.high., 1770. **£375**

Victorian Goss china mug. **£4**

Whieldon tortoiseshell teapot. **£700**

A Victorian Cadogan teapot. **£30**

Wedgwood octagonal teapot. **£175**

A Ch'ien Lung ground Canton fish tank. 18 ins. diameter. **£185**

Victorian china slop pail. **£10**

Minton majolica pot. **£8**

A Marseilles faience tureen and cover from the Veuve Perrin factory **£600**

A Cheng Te period Ming Imperial yellow bowl. £3,000 **£3,250**

A 19th century Wedgwood biscuit barrel with silver lid. **£45**

1937 Coronation Mug. **£6**

Wedgwood blue and white jasper tulip pot. **£340**

A Liverpool mug painted in famille rose colours. **£165**

A Newhall teapot. **£62**

Staffordshire salt glaze 'King of Prussia' teapot. **£225**

Wedgwood three colour dice-pattern teapot. **£270**

CHINA CABINETS & VITRINES

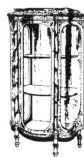

Edwardian inlaid mahogany china cabinet with glazed doors. **£85**

Edwardian mahogany display cabinet. **£65**

19th century Venetian walnut display cabinet with carved decoration. **£475**

19th century gilt display cabinet with glass shelves. **£35**

19th century black and red boulle, ormolu mounted display cabinet. **£220**

Edwardian inlaid mahogany specimen table on tapered legs. **£110**

Victorian walnut music cabinet with brass gallery. **£40**

19th century boulle credenza with ormolu mounts. **£700**

Sheraton period inlaid satinwood hanging display cabinet. **£240**

Victorian walnut display cabinet inlaid with flowers. **£200**

19th century Dutch marquetry bombe shaped display cabinet. **£3,000**

Hepplewhite period display cabinet in satinwood. **£2,750**

Edwardian inlaid mahogany display cabinet on tapered legs. **£250**

38

19th century French mahogany and tulipwood display cabinet inlaid with flowers. **£380**

19th century French display cabinet veneered in Kingwood with ormolu decoration. **£375**

Victorian display cabinet in Kingwood with Vernis Martin panels. **£750**

French walnut display cabinet inlaid with ebony. **£200**

Regency period ebonised display cabinet with figured marble top. **£185**

19th century marquetry display cabinet. **£200**

Georgian ebonised display cabinet with ormolu decoration. **£250**

Victorian burr walnut breakfront credenza. **£600**

Small Edwardian inlaid mahogany specimen display cabinet. **£95**

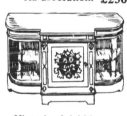

Victorian inlaid burr walnut credenza. **£500**

Chinese style Georgian mahogany display cabinet. **£600**

19th century display cabinet veneered in Kingwood with ormolu decoration. **£580**

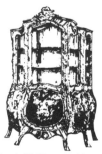

Louis Philippe cabinet with Vernis Martin panels **£2,250**

CLOCKS

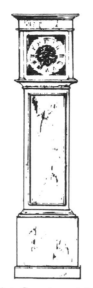

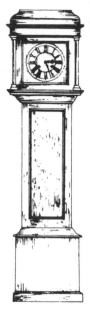

19th century Continental grandfather clock. **£250**

A late Georgian painted face oak case eight day grandfather clock. **£110**

An Edwardian oak case grandfather clock with glass panelled door. **£85**

A George III oak cased grandfather clock with square brass face. **£220**

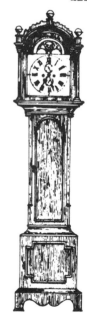

An early 18th century longcase clock in a fine burr walnut case. 7ft., high. **£850**

An 18th century longcase clock in mahogany with a fretted door. **£385**

An early German grandfather clock. **£210**

A late 18th century mahogany longcase clock with a brass silvered dial. **£300**

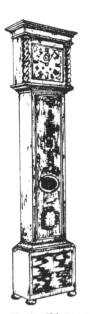

Charles II longcase clock in figured walnut case. **£900**

Late 17th century Dutch marquetry longcase clock. **£2,000**

Late Georgian figured mahogany longcase clock. **£560**

17th century marquetry cased clock by Marwick. **£1,600**

Chippendale figured mahogany longcase clock with a brass face. **£750**

Sheraton period mahogany cased grandfather clock inlaid with satinwood. **£525**

William and Mary period walnut and marquetry longcase clock by Joseph Buckingham. **£1,900**

19th century French boulle clock and pedestal 7ft. 9ins. tall. **£2,000**

CLOCKS

Late 19th century black marble mantel clock. **£10**

A Victorian 'Big Ben' picture clock. **£75**

A late 17th century bracket clock with a verge movement and engraved backplate. **£600**

A Victorian chiming bracket clock. **£110**

Victorian mahogany cased wall clock. **£70**

Regency period bracket clock in an ebonised case inlaid with brass. **£185**

A fine ebony veneered bracket clock by Joseph Knibb. **£9,500**

Late Victorian in-laid mahogany mantel clock. **£15**

A 19th century American clock in a rosewood case. **£40**

A late 18th century bracket clock in an ebonised pear-wood case. **£240**

An Edwardian mahogany cased bracket clock with an enamel dial. **£50**

19th century cuckoo
clock in a mahogany
case. **£75**

egency period mantel
ock in brass inlaid mah-
gany case. **£80**

An early 18th century
three train quarter chime
bracket clock. **£625**

An ebonised bracket
clock by James Cowan
of Edinburgh. **£750**

An early 18th century
brass lantern clock. **£450**

A George III bracket
clock 20ins.high, by
Stephen Rimbault of
London. **£1,750**

Early 19th century bracket
clock with brass face and
engraved backplate. **£300**

A Victorian lancet
case clock. **£70**

An early Victorian mantel
clock in a carved mahogany
case. **£65**

A mid 19th century
ebonised bracket clock.
£270

A fine bracket clock by Edward
East 1602-1697. **£10,000**

CLOCKS

Late 18th century Continental brass mantel clock. **£235**

Louis XV Cartel clock in ormolu and tortoise-shell by Perache of Paris. **£525**

Victorian brass mantel clock surmounted with a cherub. **£65**

A French brass carriage clock in serpentine shaped case. **£145**

19th century brass mantel clock. **£100**

A 19th century French mantel clock by Leroy et Cie of Paris. 2ft. 2ins. High. **£650**

19th century French ormolu and tortoise shell mantel clock. **£190**

A Regency period 'Father Time' clock in bronze and ormolu. **£275**

A French Empire style white marble and ormolu clock. **£140**

Louis XVI style ormolu clock with Sevres plaqu **£18**

19th century alabaster mantel clock. **£100**

A Victorian brass cased clock and barometer. **£80**

19th century French mantel clock in a green lacquered case. **£155**

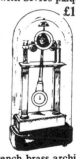

French brass architural clock, 1810. **£1**

A Louis Phillipe ormolu clock with Sevres panels. **£225**

A late Georgian wall clock in a mahogany case. **£40**

Early 19th century fusee movement wall clock with a quarter strike by Hampson of London. **£100**

A Victorian steeple clock in a mahogany case. **£24**

A fine Viennese enamel table clock 11ins. high. **£600**

Small 19th century brass carriage clock with an alarm. **£95**

19th century skeleton clock under a glass dome. **£200**

A French maritime clock in ormolu on a rouge marble base. **£300**

19th century gilded spelter mantel clock **£30**

A Louis XVI marble and ormolu clock by Piolane of Paris 22ins., high. **£365**

A 19th century brass lantern clock. **£60**

A French singing bird carriage clock 10ins. high. **£2,500**

An early 19th century French striking mantel clock. **£100**

Fine French carriage clock with alarm and repeater. **£350**

COMMODE CHESTS

Inlaid bombe shape commode with grey marble top. 3ft 5ins. wide. **£525**

19th century French commode inlaid with floral marquetry. **£575**

Georgian shaped front inlaid satinwood commode. **£2,250**

Hepplewhite shaped front commode in satinwood with doors inlaid with panels of bamboo plant designs. **£7,500**

Small French marquetry commode. **£375**

Small Italian walnut commode inlaid with satinwood. **£500**

Georgian serpentine front commode in mellow mahogany. **£750**

Louis XV petite commode in kingwood and rosewood with ormolu mounts. **£1,200**

18th century French Provencal double serpentine front commode in walnut. **£400**

17th century commode
in walnut and holly. **£1,100**

Late Georgian semi
circular commode in
satinwood inlaid with
bows and ribbons, **£675**

18th century Dutch mar-
quetry commode in yew
wood. **£800**

Dutch marquetry walnut
commode with bombe
front and sides. **£750**

Small Louis XV style
marquetry commode
on cabriole shaped
supports. **£525**

19th century kingwood
marquetry and parquetry
commode. **£650**

French commode in
kingwood and tulip-
wood with rose marble
top and ormolu decor-
ation. **£1,200**

18th century serpentine
shaped commode of
three long drawers inlaid
with various woods and
rouge marble top. **£1,000**

Georgian serpentine front
commode in satinwood
decorated with musical
instruments and ribbons.
£1,400

COMMODE AND POT CUPBOARDS

Small Victorian mahogany one step commode. £8

Victorian commode in walnut with a pull out step. £18

Late Georgian mahogany commode with lift up top and dummy drawers.
£40

Georgian mahogany commode on short square legs. £50

Regency night commode in figured mahogany on fine turned legs. £85

Victorian three step commode in mahogany.
£85

Regency bedroom cupboard in mahogany inlaid with satinwood. £70

Georgian tray top night table in satinwood inlaid with kingwood. £160

Georgian mahogany tray top commode. £85

Edwardian mahogany
bedside cupboard. £8

Mahogany and rosewood
banded square bedside
cupboard with a drawer.
£28

Mahogany circular
bedside cupboard,
2ft. 6in. high. £30

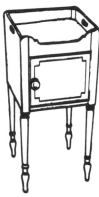

Mahogany bedside
cupboard with tray
top.   £35

Victorian mahogany
pot stand, with fluted
sides and marble top.
£35

Mahogany inlaid square
bedside stand with under-
shelf and a drawer.   £36

19th century square
tray topped bedside
cupboard.   £42

19th century satinwood
inlaid mahogany bedside
stand with tambour front.
£48

18th century mahogany
pot cupboard with a
fretted frieze.   £75

COPPER & BRASS

Victorian copper kettle and stand. **£45**

A Bidri ware brass vase. **£5**

Late Victorian brass vase 10ins. high. **£14**

Victorian copper samovar. **£30**

A large Victorian two wheel coffee mill. **£60**

Victorian brass preserving pan, 15ins. diameter. **£10**

Victorian two gallon copper milk churn. **£35**

Victorian copper milk pail. **£20**

17th century bell metal skillet. **£65**

Victorian copper skillet with iron handle. **£14**

A 19th century copper log bin. **£35**

Victorian copper helmet coal scuttle. **£45**

Victorian copper wash boiler. **£35**

19th century four gallon copper measure. **£45**

19th century small bronze howitzer. 12 ins. long. **£130**

An 18th century brass bucket. **£175**

A modern model of an early 19th century field cannon, 26ins. long. **£80**

Large Victorian bronze 'wooden wall' ships lantern, 45ins. high. **£75**

Georgian brass coal scuttle. **£30**

A Victorian brass trivet. **£12**

Victorian brass kettle. **£9**

An Art Nouveau copper jug 12 ins. high. **£10**

Victorian copper grape hod 35ins. high. **£55**

Large Georgian copper saucepan with lid. **£30**

Victorian brass milk can **£12**

Victorian brass helmet coal scuttle. **£20**

Victorian copper urn with brass tap. **£18**

Victorian copper jardiniere. **£22**

COPPER & BRASS

Victorian brass carriage lamp. **£35**

Victorian ships mast lamp in brass. **£35**

Victorian brass oil lamp with white glass shade. **£25**

Victorian brass argand lamp. **£48**

Pair of Georgian brass candlesticks 8ins., high. **£18**

Edwardian brass cash till. **£50**

Georgian brass trivet with turned wood handle. **£10**

Victorian brass and iron fire dogs. **£8**

Victorian brass students lamp. **£15**

Victorian brass inkstand. **£15**

Victorian brass fire irons complete with stand. **£40**

Victorian brass magazine stand. **£45**

17th century brass, steel handled warming pan. **£65**

Victorian brass and copper standard lamp. **£90**

Victorian ships lamp in copper. **£25**

Victorian brass table lamp. **£30**

19th century brass table lamp. **£35**

Victorian brass hanging lamp with a green glass shade. **£40**

Victorian copper chafing dish. **£20**

Victorian brass Crystal Palace bird cage. **£55**

Large Georgian copper pan. **£25**

18th century copper urn with brass lid. **£85**

Georgian brass saucepan. **£15**

Georgian brass kettle. **£18**

Georgian copper warming pan. **£45**

Victorian brass cakestand. **£28**

Large pair of brass twist candlesticks. **£18**

Victorian brass candelabrum. **£40**

CORNER CABINETS

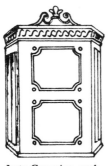

Late Georgian mahogany corner cupboard. **£90**

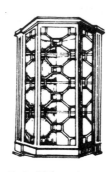

Early 18th century hanging display cabinet with astragal glazed doors and fluted pilasters. **£135**

Late Georgian walnut veneered corner cupboard. **£150**

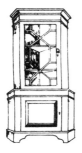

Edwardian mahogany corner cupboard. **£135**

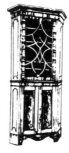

Sheraton period mahogany corner cupboard with satinwood inlay. **£425**

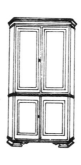

Late Georgian mahogany corner cupboard on ogee feet. **£160**

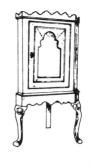

18th century walnut corner cupboard supported on carved cabriole legs. **£20(**

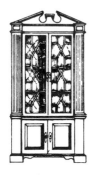

Chippendale mahogany corner cupboard with astragal glazed doors enclosing adjustable shelves. **£400**

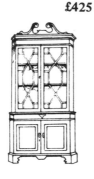

Georgian mahogany corner cupboard with centre drawer and astragal glazed doors. **£375**

18th century oak dole cupboard with centre drawer and four shelves. **£160**

Georgian mahogany corner cupboard with astragal glazed doors. **£300**

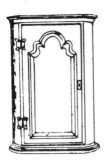

Early 18th century
black japanned cor-
ner cupboard dec-
orated with domestic
scenes. **£120**

George I walnut ven-
eered corner cupboard
with mirrored doors.
£160

Georgian bow front
mahogany corner cup-
board with pear drop
moulding. **£150**

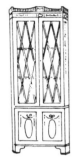

Late Georgian stand-
ng corner cupboard
n oak. **£110**

Late Georgian mah-
ogany diamond glazed
corner cupboard with
satinwood inlay. **£400**

Early Georgian walnut
corner cupboard on
stand with centre
drawer. **£425**

Queen Anne walnut
standing corner cup-
board. **£500**

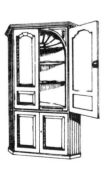

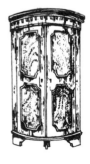

Edwardian inlaid mah-
ogany corner cupboard
with inlaid conche shell
to the lower section.
£200

Georgian stripped pine
corner cupboard. **£225**

Late Georgian finely
grained mahogany
bow fronted corner
cupboard. **£225**

George II bow fronted
corner cupboard in
mahogany. **£465**

COUCHES

Edwardian inlaid mahogany settee on square tapering legs. **£60**

Late Victorian mahogany framed love seat on turned leg supports. **£140**

Victorian ottoman on turned leg supports. **£300**

Victorian scroll end mahogany sofa on turned legs. **£95**

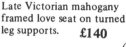

Victorian couch with carved mahogany frame on turned legs. **£125**

Victorian single end chaise longue in walnut supported on cabriole legs. **£160**

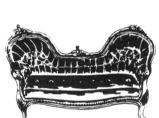

Victorian sofa in walnut on cabriole legs. **£325**

Georgian mahogany settee on cabriole legs. **£340**

Small Regency period settee in rosewood with brass mounts and brass claw feet. **£310**

Hepplewhite period mahogany settee. **£385**

Victorian ottoman with carved walnut frame supported on cabriole legs. **£425**

Edwardian ebonised
settee on tapered
legs. **£40**

Victorian mahogany
framed sofa. **£260**

Early Victorian walnut
framed buttoned couch
on cabriole legs. **£170**

Hepplewhite period
settee on tapered legs.
£440

Victorian two seater
chesterfield. **£75**

19th century gilded
day bed supported on
cabriole legs. **£325**

17th century oak
monk's bench **£220**

William IV mahogany
salon sofa. **£200**

17th century oak
settee. **£300**

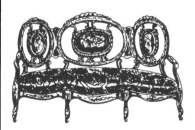

Victorian papier mache
sofa inlaid with mother
of pearl. **£500**

Early carved oak hall
seat in elm. **£200**

DAVENPORTS

Edwardian inlaid mahogany davenport with cupboard under. **£100**

William IV mahogany davehport. **£195**

Victorian inlaid walnut davenport on twist supports with two shelves under. **£85**

Victorian davenport veneered in burr walnut. **£230**

William IV mahogany davenport. **£210**

Victorian burr walnut davenport with cabriole leg front supports. **£250**

Victorian cylindrical davenport in burr walnut. **£450**

Victorian burr walnut piano top davenport with cupboard enclosing four drawers. **£425**

Chinese Chippendale style mahogany davenport. **£150**

Victorian burr walnut serpentine fronted davenport. **£260**

Regency period rosewood davenport on fluted legs. **£350**

Oriental hardwood davenport ornately carved with figures and animals. **£180**

Edwardian red mahogany davenport with cupboard enclosing four drawers. **£135**

Edwardian inlaid mahogany davenport on tapered legs with cross stretchers. **£100**

Victorian walnut davenport. **£170**

George III mahogany sliding top davenport on bracket feet. **£450**

William IV mahogany davenport with pillar supports. **£210**

Regency davenport veneered in satinwood with sliding top and pierced brass gallery. **£550**

Small Regency period davenport with oak lined drawers. **£450**

Regency mahogany sliding top davenport with four drawers. **£450**

Victorian burr walnut piano top davenport with rising top. **£400**

19th century teak military desk and stand. **£180**

Regency period writing desk and bookshelves in rosewood. **£260**

Regency rosewood davenport with sliding top and scroll feet. **£340**

DOLLS & TOYS

An early doll with muslin frock, and wool wig. **£175**

Victorian dolls house 31 x 14 x 45 ins. **£110**

Simon and Halbig doll 28ins. high. **£70**

19th century doll with original clothing. **£55**

Fine 19th century model of a horse drawn fire engine 15ins. long **£95**

Dignified doll of the late Napolean III period. **£275**

Victorian wooden horse drawn caravan 28ins. long. **£50**

A Victorian rocking horse. **£100**

Victorian china doll. **£40**

Late 19th century doll. **£25**

A rare French doll stamped Mme Rohmer. **£600**

Doll made by Armand Marseille in 1891. **£50**

A Jumeau doll with original clothes. **£125**

An early Victorian wooden pony and trap. **£80**

Victorian doll with original clothes. **£50**

Fine Victorian doll with original clothes. **£150**

Late 17th century carved and painted wooden rocking horse. **£850**

An early oak cat kennel. **£70**

19th century model of a railway signal box. **£70**

DRESSERS

18th century Welsh
dresser in oak 8ft.
long.   **£600**

Small Georgian oak
Welsh dresser with
original plate racks
4ft. 7ins. wide. **£410**

Unusually small
Georgian oak dresser
with pot board. 35
ins. wide.   **£425**

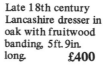

Late 18th century
Lancashire dresser in
oak with fruitwood
banding, 5ft. 9in.
long.   **£400**

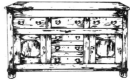

Early 18th century
oak dresser with cen-
tral cupboard. **£350**

Late Georgian oak
dresser 5ft. 7ins.
wide.   **£300**

Early Georgian oak dresser
with pot board.   **£450**

Late 17th century oak
dresser 5ft. 11ins. wide.
               £600

Late 18th century oak
dresser with pot board. **£400**

Georgian oak dresser only 4ft. 5ins. long. **£425**

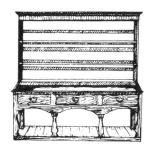

Late 17th century oak dresser with pot board. **£390**

James II oak dresser on baluster turned legs with stretchers. **£1,250**

Early 18th century polished oak dresser on ogee feet. **£425**

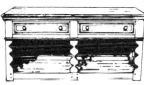

17th century oak dresser with pot board. **£460**

18th century oak dresser with spice drawers. 6ft. long. **£400**

Georgian oak dresser with fielded panels to cupboard doors. **£450**

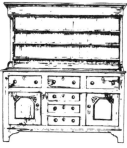

Late 18th century oak dresser with drawers and cupboards to base. 5ft., long. **£445**

George II Lancashire oak dresser. **£625**

DRESSING TABLES

Sheraton mahogany corner washstand with a centre cupboard. **£100**

Georgian mahogany dressing table with an adjustable mirror. **£450**

Late Georgian mahogany washstand with a centre drawer. **£45**

Edwardian inlaid mahogany washstand on square tapered legs. **£25**

Victorian pine washstand with a marble top and tiled splashback. **£25**

Victorian mahogany washstand on a stretcher base. **£35**

Sheraton washstand with cistern, in mahogany with boxwood stringing. **£140**

Sheraton period folding top dressing table in satinwood. **£255**

Georgian mahogany toilet cabinet. **£135**

Victorian mahogany escritoire on bun feet. **£150**

William and Mary secretaire cabinet with floral marquetry in stained and natural woods. **£1,300**

Dutch marquetry escritoire with fall front enclosing drawers and pigeon holes. **£650**

William and Mary period walnut escritoire. **£1,200**

18th century laburnum wood chest on chest. **£1,400**

French Empire ladies escritoire in mahogany. **£425**

Inlaid secretaire a abattant with fall front concealing small drawers. **£675**

Small amboyna wood escritoire on stand with a writing slide. **£375**

Reproduction French style escritoire with Sevres plaques and ormolu mounts **£475**

GLASS

Victorian opal glass vase 10ins. high. **£18**

Late Georgian cut glass decanter. **£25**

Georgian cut glass decanter. **£34**

Georgian decanter. **£15**

A Cranberry glass water jug. **£16**

An Edwardian silver mounted claret jug. **£55**

A Georgian cut glass water jug. **£27**

A Mary Gregory glass pitcher 8ins. high. **£24**

A Burmese glass jug 4ins.high. **£45**

19th century green glass wine bottle. **£12**

A Victorian glass pickle jar. **£2**

A Mildner tumbler. **£800**

Victorian red glass lustre. **£25**

19th century glass biscuit barrel. **£15**

A Mamluk enamelled glass Mosque lamp in the name of Sultan Malik Zahir Barkuk AD1382-1399. **£6,000**

An 18th century Bristol five bottle cruet. **£1,750**

A Mary Gregory glass decanter. **£30**

A Lutz glass jug. **£85**

A Tiffany Favrille vase in iridescent golden glass. **£250**

Victorian satin glass vase 7ins. high. **£16**

19th century opal glass vase **£5**

Victorian Bohemian glass flask. **£55**

A Victorian claret jug with plated mounts. **£30**

A decorative Victorian glass vase 6ins. high. **£10**

19th century Cranberry glass jug. **£15**

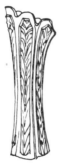

An orange Carnival glass vase. **£3**

A Victorian red glass spill vase. **£5**

An early Georgian wine bottle 10ins. high. **£18**

Silver plated decanter stand, holding three cut glass bottles. **£65**

A Victorian cut glass centrepiece. **£45**

Victorian rosewood tantalus with brass mounts containing three cut glass decanters. **£65**

A Victorian Cranberry glass fruit and flower epergne. **£35**

GLASS

Vaseline glass scent bottle. **£30**

18th century wine glass with an engraved bowl. **£475**

A Victorian glass spill vase. **£5**

A superb baluster wine glass. **£475**

A glass bowl by Gabriel Argy-Rousseau **£175**

Small Victorian coloured glass bowl. **£7.50**

A milk glass crimped bowl. **£10**

18th Century engraved wine glass. **£140**

Double ended blue overlay scent bottle with silver tops. **£35**

18th century wine glass. **£125**

Victorian red glass scent bottle with a silver top. **£18**

A mother of pearl snuff bottle. **£100**

A St. Louis green carpet ground paperweight. **£1,600**

Chinese snuff bottle. **£220**

18th century baluster
wine glass. **£145**

Victorian opal glass
vase 4ins. high. **£8**

Victorian wine glass
red. **£3.50**
blue. **£3**

A Tiffany scent
bottle. **£500**

A rare Art Nouveau
glass inkwell
£350

A Victorian water-
ing glass. **£8**

Small Victorian col-
oured glass bowl.
£5

Victorian satin glass
fruit and flower
epergne. **£40**

18th century funnel
bowl wine glass. **£150**

A blue,gilt and enamel
scent bottle with a
gilt top. **£34**

A baluster wine glass
with a trumpet bowl.
£170

Chinese overlay glass
snuff bottle. **£250**

A St. Louis fuchsia
paperweight. **£1,000**

A Peking glass-snuff
bottle with red over-
lay in the form of
flowers. **£120**

Early 18th century mahogany dressing table on squared cabriole legs.
£200

William and Mary oak dressing table.
£240

George I walnut dressing table on cabriole legs. **£375**

Georgian country made dressing table in fruitwood. **£130**

Georgian country made lowboy in oak.
£140

George I lowboy in figured walnut.
£475

William and Mary dressing table in walnut with arched frieze and turned legs with cross stretchers.
£325

Queen Anne lowboy in fruitwood supported on cabriole legs. **£550**

George II oak dressing table on squared cabriole legs.
£190

Early 19th century mahogany military chest with a secretaire drawer. **£250**

Victorian mahogany seamans chest with sunken wooden handles. **£140**

19th century military chest with brass straps and corners and iron carrying handles. **£195**

Camphor wood military chest with a secretaire drawer. **£325**

Mahogany military chest with brass straps and corners and sunken wooden knobs. **£165**

19th century mahogany military chest with a secretaire drawer. **£275**

Early 19th century teak military chest with brass straps and sunken handles. **£265**

Campaign chest in camphor wood with a helmet drawer and paw feet. **£340**

19th century camphor wood secretaire military chest with an adjustable writing slope. **£400**

Victorian carved mahogany swing mirror. **£20**

Georgian mahogany wall mirror **£90**

Regency giltwood mirror surmounted by a carved eagle **£120**

Late Georgian gilded, Adam style wall mirror. **£90**

19th century Spanish gilded mirror. **£95**

Louis XVI carved giltwood mirror. **£125**

A Hepplewhite style mahogany toilet mirror. **£55**

Late Victorian walnut dressing table mirror. **£11**

Late Victorian mahogany swing mirror. **£7**

Late Georgian mahogany swing mirror. **£55**

Late Georgian vase shaped mahogany swing mirror. **£65**

Late Georgian cheval mirror. **£60**

Victorian gilded mantel mirror. **£40**

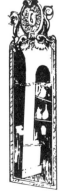

Large 19th century gilt mirror 15ft. x 4ft. **£200**

Adam style gilt
girandole. **£80**

Chippendale period wall
mirror with bird decor-
ation. **£200**

18th century carved gilt-
wood mirror. **£100**

Georgian carved and
gilded mirror. **£200**

Georgian giltwood mirror
with gesso ornamentation.
£75

Early 19th century
Spanish gilded mirror.
£95

19th century white and
gilded pine mirror. **£90**

Queen Anne lacquered
toilet mirror on a bureau
box base. **£250**

Victorian mahogany
dressing table
mirror. **£18**

Early Georgian
mahogany swing
mirror. **£85**

Late Georgian serpentine
front mahogany swing
mirror. **£65**

Early Victorian gilt wall
mirror with gesso decor-
ation. **£45**

Regency period gilded
Pier glass and table. **£250**

Late Victorian mahogany
cheval mirror. **£40**

Victorian metronome in an oak case. **£15**

26th Dynasty bronze statue of a cat. **£2,000**

Victorian brass microscope in an oak case. **£75**

A small 19th century German carved wood tankard. **£20**

A four case inro. **£225**

A bronze mare and foal by Isadore Bonheur. **£800**

Victorian chromatic stereoscope. **£15**

A 19th century oak Peg tankard. **£55**

Small pair of 18th century bellows. **£15**

Victorian turned wood tobacco jar. **£8**

Louis XV1 ormolu mounted ivory vase by Pierre Gouthlore. **£2,500**

An ivory figure of a rat. **£150**

An Infernal Harp shell from the Fringing Reef, Mauritius. **£50**

A five case inro. **£285**

Carved wood and ivory figure signed Yoshiaki, 9ins high. **£155**

Late 19th century
Officers full dress
sporran. **£45**

A bronze magicians
lamp 7½ins. tall.
£60

A rock crystal ball
mounted on a rock
crystal column,
11ins.high. **£550**

An ivory and Shaba-
yama elephant. **£550**

Victorian brass
letter scales. **£26**

19th century bronze
figure of a greyhound.
£160

A Victorian lace fan.
£8

A Scrimshaw whales
tooth. **£30**

A Shang Dynasty
archaic bronze wine
vessel. **£1,700**

A set of Victorian
brass bankers scales.
£60

A George 111 carved
walnut tobacconists
shop sign 17ins. tall.
£140

A Victorian flat iron.
£3

Large iron Tsuba
3.25ins. diameter.
£40

A Ch'ien Lung
green jade bowl.
£4,250

A sawn and polished
vug with blue and
white agate bands.
£100

MISCELLANEA

A Victorian stone garden urn 2ft.6ins.high. **£50**

A small Georgian four octave spinet 3ft7ins., wide by John Broadwood, London. 1799. **£500**

A small Regency period terrestrial globe 14ins., diameter. **£150**

A Victorian glass ship under a glass dome. 9ins., high. **£80**

Large 18th century marble fountain in the form of a swan and four cherubs. **£1,000**

Late Victorian chair steps in oak. **£25**

A Victorian Zoetrope. **£110**

A Victorian Brougham coach. **£600**

A mid Victorian baby carriage. **£55**

A 16th century Italian full suit of armour made of bright steel. **£1,500**

A Victorian stuffed bird in a glass case. **£20**

Pair of 19th century brass sugar cutters. **£25**

A Victorian bamboo hall stand. **£30**

A Georgian mahogany Butlers tray and stand. **£100**

A Victorian cutlery cleaner. **£25**

19th century ironwork plant stand. **£18**

A late Victorian pottery elephant oil lamp 24ins., high. **£100**

A Flemish two manual harpsichord by Hans the Younger, circa 1690 **£9,600**

Pair of late Georgian library steps. **£150**

Large Scottish spinning wheel in oak and pine. **£55**

Fine quality Gypsy Queen caravan. **£950**

A mahogany hoddmeter by Dolland of London. **£125**

MODELS

Prisoner of War bone
model of H.M.S.Mars
£2,000

A working model of
a piston with flywheel.
£35

French Prisoner of War
model of the frigate
Venus circa 1815.
£900

19th century scale model of
a steam tug.   **£225**

A model of the North
Eastern 1849 type Kitson
Thompson and Hewitson
Leeds 2.4.0. Locomotive.
£800

A coal fired working model
of the old LMS locomotive
Highland Chief.   **£350**

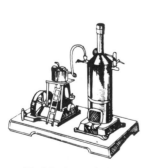

Model of a vertical
stationary steam engine
13ins. high.   **£60**

A Victorian model of a galleon.

£25

A 19th century coal fired
model steam engine 13½ins.
high.   **£90**

19th century poly-
phone in a walnut case.
£300

A Victorian penny in
the slot polyphone.
£850

A Victorian Swiss
musical box in a
rosewood case. **£400**

An Edison Standard
phonograph. **£85**

A late 19th century
gramophone with a
fine brass horn. **£85**

A Victorian musical
box by Robert
F. Knoeloch play-
ing ten airs. **£450**

An animated snake
dancer with a
musical movement by
Decamps of Paris.
£1,600

A 19th century French auto-
maton group depicting a
barbers shop. **£1,400**

A 19th century sing-
ing bird in a cage
£260

A 19th century automated
Spanish dancer. **£700**

A Victorian anim-
ated bisque
headed doll. **£700**

Victorian mahogany pedestal desk with a cylinder top. **£150**

Chippendale mahogany kneehole desk on bracket feet. **£550**

Victorian mahogany pedestal desk. **£145**

Late Georgian satinwood kneehole desk. **£675**

Georgian mahogany pedestal desk with pigeon holes and drawers enclosed by a tambour shutter. **£500**

Chippendale mahogany kneehole desk on ogee feet, with writing slide **£800**

Sheraton mahogany kneehole desk. **£600**

William and Mary walnut kneehole desk with ebony arabesque marquetry inlay. **£1,400**

George I walnut kneehole desk with recessed cupboard 2ft9ins., wide. **£1,200**

Regency period padouk wood pedestal desk with brass edging to the top. **£260**

19th century mahogany pedestal desk. **£170**

Victorian oak pedestal desk. **£100**

Victorian mahogany pedestal desk with brass drop handles. **£160**

Military style camphor wood pedestal desk with brass handles and fitted top drawer. **£425**

Chippendale period mahogany serpentine front kneehole desk. **£1,600**

Sheraton inlaid satinwood kneehole desk. **£1,100**

Late Georgian inlaid mahogany kneehole desk. **£410**

Queen Anne kneehole desk in walnut with a frieze drawer in the top moulding. **£2,300**

SECRETAIRES

Georgian mahogany serpentine front chest. **£800**

Chippendale figured mahogany secretaire. **£350**

Hepplewhite secretaire chest in mahogany on splay feet. **£300**

19th century mahogany secretaire bookcase of inlaid satinwood with boxwood stringing. **£500**

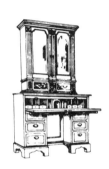

Georgian mahogany chest with secretaire drawer and cupboard top. **£450**

18th century serpentine front walnut writing cabinet. **£1,800**

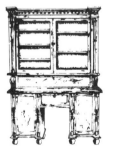

William IV mahogany secretaire bookcase. **£325**

Hepplewhite style secretaire bookcase in mahogany with glazed doors. **£525**

Sheraton style secretaire bookcase in mahogany with astragal glazed doors. **£535**

19th century brass banded mahogany secretaire. **£200**

Georgian mahogany serpentine front secretaire chest, 40ins. wide. **£410**

Late Victorian mahogany secretaire chest on bun feet, 3ft. 6ins. wide. **£85**

Georgian mahogany secretaire bookcase 4ft. wide. **£525**

Regency mahogany secretaire bookcase veneered in zebra wood. **£1,600**

Georgian tallboy in mahogany with secretaire drawer having canted corners and ogee feet. **£510**

Hepplewhite mahogany secretaire bookcase with cupboards below. **£675**

Fine secretaire bookcase in satinwood inlaid with urns and flowers. **£3,000**

Chippendale mahogany secretaire bookcase with shaped pediment and ogee feet. **£1,300**

Edwardian red mahogany sideboard. **£90**

Early Victorian mahogany pedestal sideboard inlaid with ebony. **£120**

Sheraton mahogany break-front sideboard with satin-wood inlay. **£500**

Georgian mahogany bow fronted sideboard 5ft.9ins., wide. **£400**

Late Georgian mahogany sideboard with a tambour front cupboard. **£525**

Late Georgian concave front mahogany sideboard. **£375**

Regency period maple and satinwood sideboard inlaid with ebony. **£425**

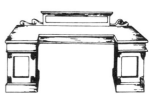

Adam period mahogany sideboard on fine turned legs. **£440**

Early Victorian mahogany pedestal sideboard. **£85**

Hepplewhite mahogany
sideboard with a serp-
entine shaped front. **£550**

Late Victorian rosewood
sideboard inlaid with bone
and ivory. **£160**

Georgian mahogany
sideboard 5ft6ins.wide.
£400

Early 19th century small
inverted breakfront
sideboard in mahogany
5ft. wide. **£350**

Edwardian mahogany
sideboard. **£75**

Regency period mahogany
sideboard on fine turned
legs. **£245**

Sheraton period serpentine
fronted sideboard in finely
grained mahogany. **£1,500**

George III mahogany sideboard
inlaid and crossbanded in satinwood 5ft 3ins., wide. **£700**

Regency period mahogany
sideboard on paw feet. **£375**

85

Silver coffee pot, London 1771. **£1,100**

George I plain cylindrical pot by Simon Pantin 1723, 28 oz. **£2,350**

George III silver coffee pot by George Smith and Thomas Hayter, London 1795. **£520**

Chocolate pot by Isaac Cooksen, Newcastle 1732. **£1,500**

George II Channel Islands hot milk jug by Guillaume Hardy Guernsey 1740. 9 oz. **£1,750**

George I plain bullet shaped teapot by Isaac Liger 1724, 13 oz. **£850**

Victorian plated teapot. **£8**

A silver gilt mounted, frosted glass wine jug by Charles and George Fox 1856. **£150**

A helmet shaped ewer with the full Royal armorials of Queen Anne by Thomas Boulton Dublin 1702, 47oz. **£6,250**

A Victorian plated cream jug. **£12**

George II plain pear shaped jug by David Willaume Jnr. 1730, 35 oz. **£6,250**

A George II flagon by Richard Bayley, 1737 **£825**

Beaker by Wakelin and Garrard London 1802, 3 oz. **£120**

Christening mug, London 1846. **£40**

Charles II beaker, London 1676. **£1,100**

George II coffee pot by John Chapman of London 1735, 27½oz. **£525**

George III silver coffee jug by Burwash and Sibley, London 1805, 25oz. **£200**

Swedish coffee pot by Anders Castem of Eksjo 1775. **£3,600**

Victorian coffee pot, 1845. **£575**

Victorian silver teapot, 18 oz. **£50**

George II bullet shaped teapot by Lewis Pantin, 1783 **£1,800**

George III silver teapot, 1818. **£115**

Cream jug by William King, London, 1768, 2½ oz. **£85**

George II silver jug by Charles Kandler, 1730, 52 oz. **£3,150**

Silver milk jug by Hester Bateman, 1786. **£180**

A William and Mary silver ewer, 1690. **£1,100**

Queen Anne mug, London 1702. **£400**

Christening mug, Birmingham 1861. **£40**

An Irish tankard, 1690. **£525**

A German silver tankard by Ulrich Schonmacher, 1580. **£1,850**

SILVER

George III sauceboat by
John Harris. **£165**

A reproduction George III
sauceboat. **£95**

George II sauceboat. **£225**

Victorian grape scissors.
£22

Georgian sugar tongs.
£14

Georgian sugar nips.
£20

Silver sifter spoon. London
1838. **£14**

Silver cruet with cut
glass bottles. 1828. **£150**

Victorian egg cruet by
George Fox 1865. **£700**

A Victorian silver egg
cruet. 24oz. **£115**

George III Irish sweet-
meat basket,1794. 8½oz.
£210

Pierced sweet basket with
a blue glass liner,1844. **£90**

Victorian silver cake basket,
16 oz. **£65**

Victorian silver sweet
bowl, 6oz. **£35**

Silver punch bowl
Guernsey 1700. **£3,500**

Hexagonal silver gilt
sweet bowl,1933. **£65**

George III chamber-stick, 1818, 9 oz. **£115**

George III chamber-stick, 1801, 8 oz. **£145**

George IV chamber-stick Sheffield 1828, 10 oz. **£115**

Heart shaped caddy spoon 1825. **£35**

George III caddy spoon, 1802. **£25**

Bright cut caddy spoon, Birmingham 1822. **£26**

Victorian leaf shaped caddy spoon. **£30**

Late Georgian plated tea caddy. **£15**

Set of three silver tea caddies by John Chivers of Birmingham. **£1,800**

Victorian silver tea caddy 1890, 11 oz. **£40**

Victorian plated inkwell. **£15**

Victorian plated inkstand. **£30**

George III silver ink-stand by Samuel Hennell, London 1813, 67oz. **£1,750**

A Russian soup tureen cover and stand. **£1,000**

An Italo-French soup tureen and cover by J. Beya, 1762. **£4,500**

Soup tureen and cover by Digby Scott and Benjamin Smith, 1804, 324oz. **£1,400**

SILVER

George III silver
salt **£45**

Victorian silver
mustard pot with
a blue glass liner.
£40

Silver mustard
pot by John Emes
1803. **£65**

A Victorian silver
vase, 6 oz. **£20**

A stirrup cup in the form
of a hares mask by Emes
and Barnard 1809, 11oz
£1,100

Silver cup 1917
11 oz. **£40**

Two handled silver
cup and cover by
Paul de Lamerie
1737, 56 oz. **£3,500**

George II spirit kettle
by Thomas Wright,
1754, 64 oz. **£450**

Sheffield plate spirit
kettle and stand,
1860. **£75**

Kettle and stand by
Ayme Videau, London
1735. **£525**

Victorian silver
brandy warmer. **£100**

Victorian plated
brandy warmer. **£20**

Silver brandy warmer
1937. **£110**

Small Victorian
vinaigrette. **£50**

Victorian snuff box
1844. **£85**

Victorian silver
match case. **£8**

Victorian plated syphon holder. **£8**

George III silver gilt wine cooler by Paul Storr 1813. **£1,500**

Sheffield plated wine cooler. **£100**

Silver pepper caster, 1911. **£40**

Victorian silver sugar caster, 4oz. **£30**

Sugar caster by Simon Pantin, 1716. **£800**

Silver caster by P.and W. Bateman, London, 1807. 3oz. **£160**

George II silver salver London. 1759. 12½oz. **£300** **£275**

George III silver snuffer tray. London 1775. **£110**

George III coaster by Peter and Anne Bateman, London 1798. **£115**

Victorian silver smokers companion. **£38**

Victorian silver frame. **£25**

An Italian casket shaped foot warmer, 1730. **£2,800**

George III silver bell. **£240**

Victorian silver nurses buckle. **£10**

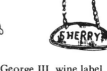

George III wine label, 1790. **£18**

Silver napkin ring. 1910. **£5**

STANDS

Victorian mahogany lamp stand with spiral pillar, 122cm. high. **£18**

Victorian mahogany lamp stand on tripod feet, 3ft. 11in. **£18**

19th century pair of Japanese red lacquer fan shaped trays on a bamboo stand, 54cm. wide. **£26**

Late 19th century carved oak hallstand with mirror and glove box, 3ft. wide. **£34**

Bamboo plant stand with tiled top, circa 1900. **£40**

Oval rosewood jardiniere stand with brass gallery and ormolu mounted feet. **£50**

Chinese carved padouk wood jardiniere stand, 2ft. high. **£60**

Oval rosewood ormolu mounted plant pedestal with kingwood frieze. **£90**

Round cistern stand with marble top, carved legs, frieze and undershelf. **£100**

Ebony jardiniere, with carved circular top and trunk patterned stem, 3ft. 3in. high. **£150**

19th century figured walnut pedestal. **£200**

18th century mahogany wine-lectern table with adjustable height. **£225**

Round gueridon with mosaic marble top, standing on four fluted, tapered legs. **£270**

18th century mahogany easel table on pad feet. **£275**

Continental carved wood cherub plant holder. **£310**

Regency rosewood music stand with reeded legs. **£350**

One of a pair of George III mahogany diningroom urns and pedestals. **£682**

Regency folio stand. **£1,200**

STOOLS

Victorian mahogany revolving piano stool on platform base. **£25**

Victorian revolving piano stool in rosewood on paw feet. **£48**

Victorian revolving piano stool in papier mache. **£50**

Regency period revolving piano stool. **£85**

Victorian footstool with a beadwork cover. **£15**

Victorian walnut footstool on bun feet. **£12**

Regency period footstool in rosewood. **£40**

Victorian mahogany footstool. **£8**

Georgian stool with cluster column legs. **£140**

Regency period carved giltwood footstool. **£150**

Tudor period oak joined stool. **£225**

Hepplewhite mahogany stool on reeded legs. **£100**

Hepplewhite mahogany window seat. **£185**

William and Mary footstool in walnut. **£285**

Edwardian inlaid mahogany suite
on square tapering legs with spade
feet.   **£140**

Edwardian ebonised suite with carved
backs and tapered legs.   **£110**

Victorian button back suite with
carved rosewood frames on cabriole
leg supports.   **£370**

Louis XV style giltwood drawing
room suite.   **£550**

TABLES

Victorian walnut chess table on a platform base. **£40**

Victorian black lacquered table inlaid with ivory. **£45**

19th century Japanese lacquer table with mother of pearl inlay. **£60**

Victorian bamboo pot stand. **£1**

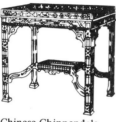

Chinese Chippendale mahogany serving table. **£135**

Victorian mahogany cutlery stand. **£20**

Small Sheraton mahogany drum table on tapered legs with cross stretchers. **£210**

Small early 19th century mahogany drum table. **£150**

Victorian mahogany adjustable music stand. **£40**

Edwardian dark mahogany occasional table. **£45**

Victorian occasional table in rosewood. **£40**

18th century elm cricket table with shelf. **£75**

Adam style satinwood tricoteuse inlaid with garlands of flowers. **£275**

Louis XV ormolu mounted consol table with a marble top. **£2,600**

Georgian mahogany tea table on a tripod base. **£135**

Victorian walnut Gypsy table. **£15**

Early 19th century gilded tripod table with brass gallery. **£75**

Louis Philippe etagere in kingwood with Sevres plaques. **£350**

Victorian games table in walnut on a stretcher base. **£60**

Victorian mahogany bedside table. **£22**

Late Georgian mahogany architects table. **£265**

Syrian hardwood folding table inlaid with brass. **£15**

George III table with a painted porcelain top and ormolu mounts. **£350**

Victorian inlaid burr walnut tripod table 20ins., diameter. **£70**

Charles II folding table in oak with plain turned legs. **£300**

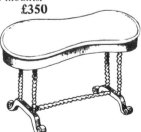

Victorian papier mache tip top table. **£95**

Victorian walnut stretcher table. **£65**

Regency period mahogany table with a parquetry top. **£225**

TABLES

Regency rosewood card table crossbanded in satinwood. **£170**

Edwardian inlaid mahogany envelope card table. **£135**

Early Victorian rosewood card table with a beaded frieze. **£135**

Hepplewhite mahogany card table on tapered legs. **£225**

Regency rosewood card table with brass inlaid decoration. **£280**

Victorian inlaid burr walnut card table. **£170**

Regency mahogany card table on fluted legs, inlaid with satinwood. **£135**

Georgian concertina action tea table in mahogany on carved cabriole legs. **£375**

Chippendale mahogany card table with gadrooned frieze on square legs chamfered on the inside edge. **£210**

Queen Anne folding top walnut card table. **£550**

19th century boulle flap top card table with ormolu decoration. **£350**

Queen Anne folding table inlaid with flowers, on carved cabriole legs. **£600**

Regency supper table in rosewood with a cross-banded top. **£200**

Sheraton Pembroke table in satinwood, crossbanded in rosewood. **£475**

William and Mary oak gateleg table. **£300**

Victorian stripped pine Pembroke table. **£20**

George III red walnut drop leaf dining table with club legs and pad feet. **£225**

Victorian mahogany supper table. **£110**

Late Georgian mahogany Pembroke table with box-wood stringing, on tapered legs. **£120**

Late 18th century mahogany club foot envelope table. **£210**

Georgian oak drop leaf cottage dining table. **£60**

Small Edwardian inlaid mahogany Sutherland table. **£50**

Regency mahogany dining table with concertina action, on turned and reeded legs. **£210**

Victorian burr walnut Sutherland table with oval leaves. **£115**

Regency sofa table with a crossbanded top, on lyre shaped supports. **£750**

18th century mahogany sofa table with D shaped leaves and crossbanded top. **£850**

Regency brass inlaid pedestal sofa table in rosewood. **£550**

Regency mahogany sofa table with a tooled leather top and flaps. **£475**

Regency rosewood sofa table crossbanded in satinwood with inlaid brass stringing. **£475**

Small mahogany sofa table on umbrella leg supports. **£500**

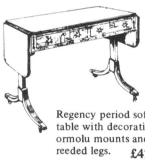

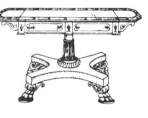

Regency period sofa table with decorative ormolu mounts and reeded legs. **£425**

Brass inlaid Regency sofa table in rosewood. **£700**

Regency ebonised sofa table with brass inlay. **£400**

Regency pedestal sofa table in mahogany, the edges and legs inlaid with coromandel wood. **£400**

Regency rosewood sofa table with crossbanded top on a stretcher base. **£465**

Regency rosewood sofa table with turned supports and splay feet. **£500**

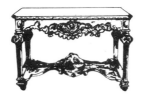

Robert Adam giltwood side table. **£450**

Italian carved walnut side table with pink marble top. **£310**

Late 17th century Dutch table in laburnam wood. **£750**

Regency pier table on tapered legs extensively decorated with curled paperwork of flowers and leaf designs. **£1,500**

Early 18th century Italian walnut side table. **£235**

William and Mary oak side table. **£155**

Elizabethan serving table in oak. **£360**

Small red boulle side table with ormolu mounts. **£210**

Victorian mahogany stretcher table. **£60**

Regency mahogany consol table with dolphin front supports and brass gallery. **£500**

Cromwellian oak side table. **£325**

Carved and gilded Louis XV consol table with a figured marble top. **£540**

TABLES

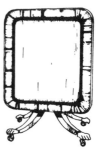

Regency centre table with a crossbanded rosewood top. **£520**

Georgian mahogany supper table, the top carved with acanthus and shell ornament. **£240**

Regency rosewood, crossbanded breakfast table with brass claw feet. **£500**

Late Victorian mahogany centre table on platform base. **£75**

Regency mahogany drum table on tripod base with carved feet. **£600**

Victorian burr walnut loo table on a centre column with cabriole shaped feet. **£170**

Late Victorian inlaid walnut loo table. **£100**

George II table and side table on carved cabriole legs with ball and claw feet. **£425**

William IV mahogany table on a centre column with paw feet. **£110**

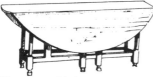

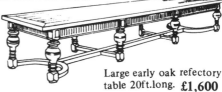

Irish wakes table in cherry wood. **£475**

Large early oak refectory table 20ft.long. **£1,600**

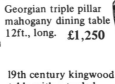

Georgian triple pillar mahogany dining table 12ft., long. **£1,250**

19th century kingwood table with a tooled leather top. **£500**

Regency brass inlaid centre table in rosewood. **£875**

Victorian mahogany centre table on a platform base with paw feet. **£90**

Victorian quarter veneered centre table in mahogany. **£150**

Victorian burr walnut marquetry loo table inlaid with birds and flowers. **£700**

18th century mahogany table on a carved tripod base. **£145**

Late Victorian walnut table inlaid with ebony. **£125**

Regency period rosewood drum top library table. 4ft diameter, **£900**

Large 17th century oak dining table. **£500**

18th century mahogany drum table. **£900**

Regency mahogany two pillar dining table. **£450**

Victorian mahogany telescope dining table. **£65**

Late 18th century sectional dining table in mahogany. **£425**

Early 17th century oak draw leaf table. **£750**

TEA CADDIES & BOXES

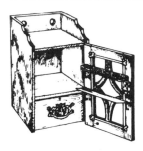

Victorian oak smokers companion. **£12**

Georgian mahogany cutlery urn. **£125**

Georgian mahogany apothecary box. **£18**

Regency period camphorwood writing slope. **£65**

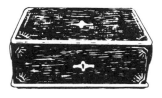

A brass bound Regency rosewood toilet box with fitted interior. **£55**

Victorian walnut writers companion. **£20**

Small early 19th century inlaid mahogany tea caddy. **£30**

George III mahogany table coaster. **£80**

Victorian parquetry tea caddy with a glass liner. **£40**

Regency mahogany specimen box. **£140**

A Victorian biscuit tin. **£6**

Victorian walnut card box with brass fittings. **£16**

Regency rosewood
writing slope. **£35**

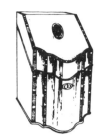

Late Georgian inlaid mahogany knife box. **£65**

Late Georgian apothecary box complete with bottles. **£65**

A Tunbridge ware writing slope. **£50**

A Victorian vanity case in coromandel wood with silver fittings. **£70**

Victorian mahogany cutlery box with a brass carrying handle. **£15**

A Tunbridge ware jewellery box. **£20**

A Georgian mahogany cheese coaster. **£50**

A small 19th century pony skin trunk. **£34**

Victorian games box in walnut. **£75**

Georgian mahogany apothecary box. **£70**

Regency period brass inlaid rosewood tea caddy with glass liner. **£45**

TRUNKS

17th century oak mule
chest. **£170**

17th century steel band-
ed treasure chest. **£285**

Georgian mahogany
silver chest. **£130**

18th century Spanish
carved walnut coffer.
£325

17th century oak bible
box. **£135**

Carolean oak dower
chest with panelled
front. **£120**

16th century oak
hutch. **£500**

Elizabethan oak trav-
elling desk. **£90**

17th century beechwood
bread trough. **£155**

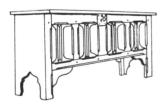

Tudor oak joined dower
chest. **£400**

Victorian mahogany
sarcophagus shaped
cellarette. **£100**

Flemish Gothic buffet
in elm. Circa 1500. **£750**

Brass bound camphor wood trunk with brass carrying handles. **£70**

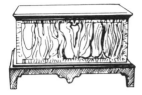

18th century walnut chest decorated with herring-bone inlay. **£175**

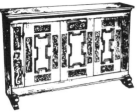

19th century German ebonised cabinet of Baroque influence on carved scroll feet 7ft.5ins.wide. **£1,600**

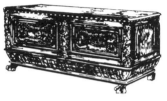

16th century Italian cassone in carved walnut 4ft.10ins., wide. **£425**

18th century elm dough bin on square legs with stretchers. **£95**

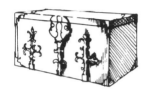

17th century French cassette containing a multitude of secret drawers. **£275**

17th century iron treasure chest, the internal lock mechanism with eight moving catches. **£325**

Late 17th century oak box on stand. **£140**

William and Mary period lacquered chest on stand. **£600**

Georgian country made oak bible box. **£165**

16th century oak bible box. **£50**

Late 17th century oak chest 4ft 2ins.,wide. **£200**

WARDROBES & CUPBOARDS

Early 18th century oak clothes press. **£225**

Mid 17th century oak livery cupboard. **£320**

Georgian oak cupboard with four drawers to the lower section. **£200**

French provencal armoire in walnut. **£400**

17th century oak livery cupboard with panelled doors. **£350**

Victorian stripped pine wardrobe. **£25**

Early 17th century French cupboard in oak. **£350**

17th century oak cupboard. **£650**

17th century oak court cupboard. **£475**

French provencal armoire in walnut on carved cabriole legs. **£275**

Late Georgian finely grained mahogany breakfront wardrobe **£200**

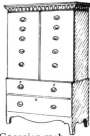

Late Georgian mahogany clothes press with mock drawers to the upper section. **£145**

18th century French provencal carved oak armoire with steel fittings. **£350**

Late Georgian mahogany wardrobe with panelled doors and two drawers to the base. **£100**

Small William IV mahogany cabinet with a centre drawer. **£100**

Georgian oak collectors cabinet with key pattern frieze. **£250**

17th century oak court cupboard. **£500**

17th century oak clothes press with two drawers. **£310**

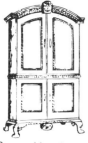

George 11 mahogany cupboard on carved cabriole legs. **£260**

Elizabethan oak court cupboard. **£650**

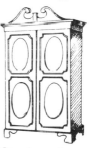

Late Georgian mahogany hanging wardrobe. **£155**

18th century Dutch marquetry wardrobe. **£1,600**

Early 18th century oak cupboard. **£385**

Georgian mahogany linen press on splayed feet. **£110**

109

WHATNOTS

Victorian inlaid walnut three tier whatnot. **£65**

William IV rosewood whatnot with twist supports. **£100**

Victorian inlaid walnut corner whatnot. **£50**

Late Georgian two tier whatnot in mahogany. **£125**

Regency whatnot in rosewood. **£160**

Regency four tier whatnot in mahogany. **£90**

Early Victorian burr walnut whatnot. **£120**

Sheraton mahogany whatnot with simulated bamboo supports. **£140**

19th century red boulle etagere. **£135**

19th century marquetry etagere. **£145**

A Regency period rosewood whatnot. **£170**

Hepplewhite mahogany whatnot. **£160**

Early Victorian mahogany whatnot. **£130**

Sheraton mahogany whatnot with two drawers. **£175**

Georgian mahogany whatnot with cupboard base. **£145**

Sheraton cellarette of finely figured mahogany. **£210**

George III mahogany brass bound wine cooler. **£325**

George III mahogany cellarette on stand with brass carrying handles. **£200**

Georgian mahogany domed top wine cooler on square tapered legs. **£190**

18th century brass bound octagonal wine cooler in mahogany. **£325**

Chippendale mahogany cellarette with original decanters. **£345**

William IV wine cooler of figured mahogany on paw feet. **£150**

Hepplewhite oval cellarette in mahogany. **£300**

Sheraton mahogany wine cooler 22ins. wide. **£260**

Chippendale oval mahogany brass bound cellarette. **£225**

Sheraton mahogany cellarette on turned leg supports. **£200**

Sheraton period figured mahogany wine cooler inlaid with satinwood. **£600**

Late Regency rosewood teapoy inlaid with mother of pearl. **£130**

Victorian burr walnut octagonal work box on carved cabriole legs. **£85**

Tunbridge ware workbox on splay feet with brass claw castors. **£325**

Regency work table in yew wood on a turned centre column and brass paw feet. **£160**

Victorian mahogany folding top work table on a shaped platform with bun feet. **£130**

Victorian burr walnut sewing table on stretcher base with carved cabriole legs. **£145**

Victorian walnut workbox with a chess board top. **£110**

Regency figured mahogany work table supported on carved splay feet. **£225**

Victorian sewing table in rosewood on a stretcher base. **£125**

Early Victorian burr walnut work table with drop flaps. **£165**

Victorian work table in mahogany on a centre column with platform base. **£130**

Victorian mahogany teapoy on a shaped platform base. **£95**

Victorian papier mache teapoy inlaid with mother of pearl. **£130**

Regency period brass inlaid rosewood teapoy. **£260**

Victorian teapoy in pollard oak on twist column supports and carved cabriole legs. **£100**

Victorian burr walnut work table with a chess board top. **£175**

Marquetry work table on turned legs with a single drawer and drop flaps. **£165**

Regency mahogany work table on turned column supports and stretcher base. **£150**

Victorian mahogany work table on turned legs. **£90**

Victorian mahogany work table on a centre column with shaped platform base. **£100**

Sheraton mahogany sewing table crossbanded in partridgewood. **£250**

Edwardian inlaid mahogany sewing table. **£75**

WRITING TABLES

George III marquetry writing table. **£500**

19th century bureau plat in kingwood with ormolu mounts. **£1,000**

French walnut desk on cabriole legs with ormolu mounts and Sevres panels. **£550**

19th century inlaid satinwood bonheur de jour. **£725**

Regency rosewood library table with lyre end supports. **£435**

19th century boulle writing cabinet. **£540**

Louis XVI giltwood writing table with an adjustable centre flap. **£850**

Georgian walnut writing table. **£575**

Edwardian satinwood decorated writing table. **£260**

Georgian mahogany Carlton House writing table. **£750**

Victorian mahogany writing table with carved cabriole legs. **£125**

Louis XV style marquetry writing table with an adjustable writing slope to the centre. **£650**

Georgian Pembroke writing table with rise and fall secretaire. **£400**

18th century tambour desk with mock drawers in back and sides. 4ft.2ins., long. **£475**

Sheraton satinwood writing desk on tapered legs. **£500**

Edwardian mahogany table desk crossbanded in satinwood. **£80**

George III cylinder fronted mahogany secretaire. 3ft. 4ins. wide. **£385**

Victorian rosewood library table on a stretcher base. **£115**

Empire style mahogany bureau a cylindre with pierced brass gallery and marble top. 4ft6ins., wide. **£450**

Regency period rosewood writing table with drawers to the front, and pierced brass gallery. **£225**

Edwardian Hepplewhite style inlaid mahogany writing table. **£125**

Late Georgian satinwood and rosewood writing table. **£650**

19th century inlaid satinwood writing table. **£425**

Edwardian inlaid mahogany writing table. **£80**

CHAIR BACKS

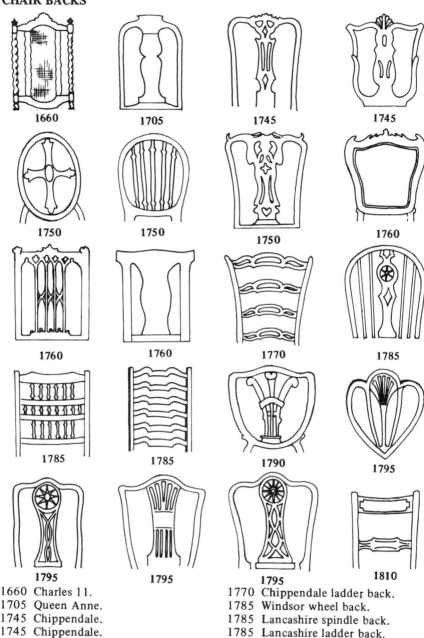

1660

1705

1745

1745

1750

1750

1750

1760

1760

1760

1770

1785

1785

1785

1790

1795

1795

1795

1795

1810

1660 Charles 11.
1705 Queen Anne.
1745 Chippendale.
1745 Chippendale.
1750 Georgian.
1750 Hepplewhite.
1750 Chippendale.
1760 French Rococo.
1760 Gothic.
1760 Splat back.

1770 Chippendale ladder back.
1785 Windsor wheel back.
1785 Lancashire spindle back.
1785 Lancashire ladder back.
1790 Shield and feathers.
1795 Shield back.
1795 Hepplewhite.
1795 Hepplewhite camel back.
1795 Hepplewhite.
1810 Late Georgian bar back.

1810
1810
1815
1815

1820
1820
1820
1825

1830
1830
1830
1830

1835
1840
1845
1845

1850
1860
1870
1875

1810 Thomas Hope 'X' frame.
1810 Regency rope back.
1815 Regency.
1815 Regency cane back.
1820 Regency.
1820 Empire.
1820 Regency bar back.
1825 Regency bar back.
1830 Regency bar back.
1830 Bar back.

1830 William IV bar back.
1830 William IV.
1835 Lath back.
1840 Victorian balloon back.
1845 Victorian.
1845 Victorian bar back.
1850 Victorian.
1860 Victorian.
1870 Victorian.
1875 Cane back.

FEET

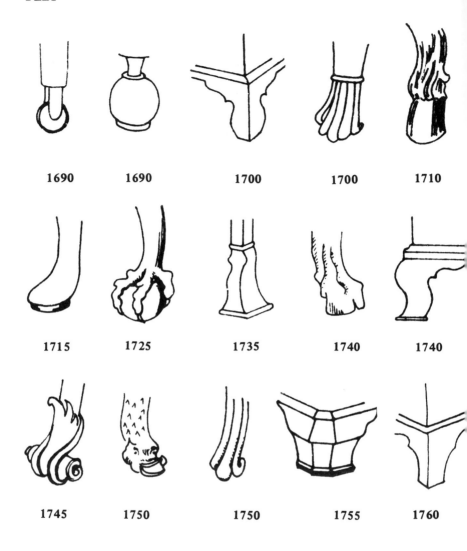

| 1690 | 1690 | 1700 | 1700 | 1710 |

| 1715 | 1725 | 1735 | 1740 | 1740 |

| 1745 | 1750 | 1750 | 1755 | 1760 |

1690 Wooden Wheel
1690 Ball
1700 Bracket
1700 Spanish
1710 Hoog
1715 Pad
1725 Ball and Claw
1735 Cabriole Leg Foot

1740 Stylised Hoof
1740 Ogee
1745 French Knurl
1750 Dolphin
1750 English Knurl
1755 Elaborate Bracket
1760 Splay

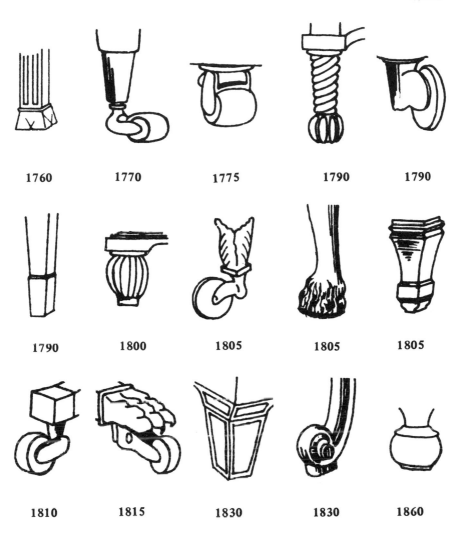

1760	1770	1775	1790	1790
1790	1800	1805	1805	1805
1810	1815	1830	1830	1860

1760 Gutta Foot
1770 Tapered Socket
1775 Peg and Plate
1790 Spiral Twist
1790 Wheel Castor
1790 Spade
1800 Fluted Ball
1805 Decorative Socket

1805 Paw
1805 Regency
1810 Horizontal Socket
1815 Lions Paw
1830 Regency
1830 Victorian Scroll
1860 Victorian Bun

119

HANDLES

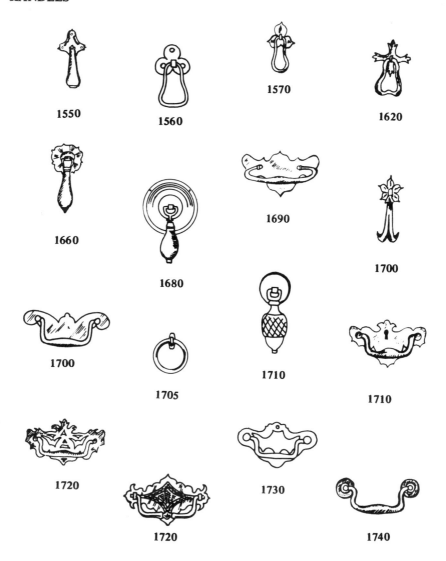

1550
1560
1570
1620
1660
1680
1690
1700
1700
1705
1710
1710
1720
1720
1730
1740

1550 Tudor drop handle.
1560 Early Stuart loop.
1570 Early Stuart loop.
1620 Early Stuart loop.
1660 Stuart drop.
1680 Stuart drop.
1690 William & Mary solid backplate.
1700 William & Mary split tail.

1700 Queen Anne solid backplate.
1705 Queen Anne ring.
1710 Acorn drop.
1710 Queen Anne loop.
1720 Early Georgian pierced.
1720 Early Georgian brass drop.
1730 Cut away backplate.
1740 Georgian plain brass loop.

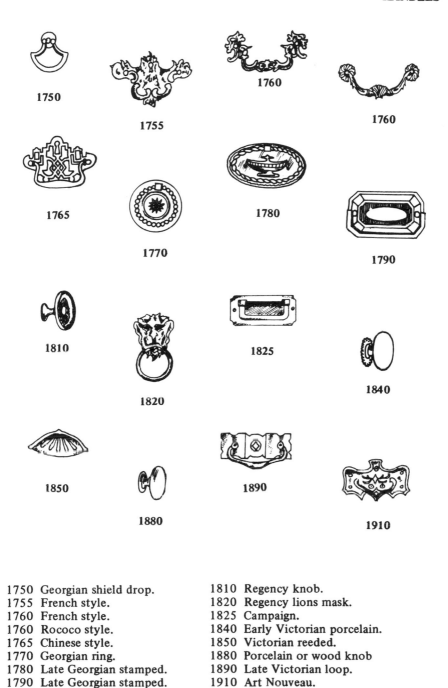

1750 Georgian shield drop.
1755 French style.
1760 French style.
1760 Rococo style.
1765 Chinese style.
1770 Georgian ring.
1780 Late Georgian stamped.
1790 Late Georgian stamped.

1810 Regency knob.
1820 Regency lions mask.
1825 Campaign.
1840 Early Victorian porcelain.
1850 Victorian reeded.
1880 Porcelain or wood knob
1890 Late Victorian loop.
1910 Art Nouveau.

LEGS

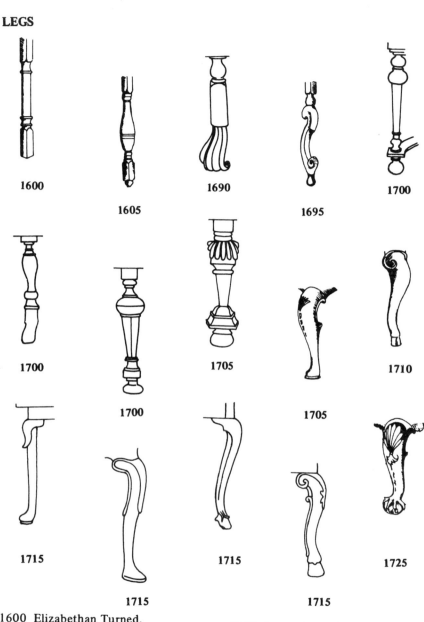

1600

1605

1690

1695

1700

1700

1700

1705

1705

1710

1715

1715

1715

1725

1715

1715

1600 Elizabethan Turned.
1605 Stuart Baluster
1690 Spanish
1695 William and Mary 'S' Curve.
1700 Trumpet
1700 Portugese Bulb.
1700 Mushroom.
1705 Inverted Cup.

1705 Queen Anne Cabriole.
1710 Hoof Foot.
1715 Modified Cabriole.
1715 Pad Foot.
1715 Cabriole.
1715 Hoof.
1725 Ball and Claw.

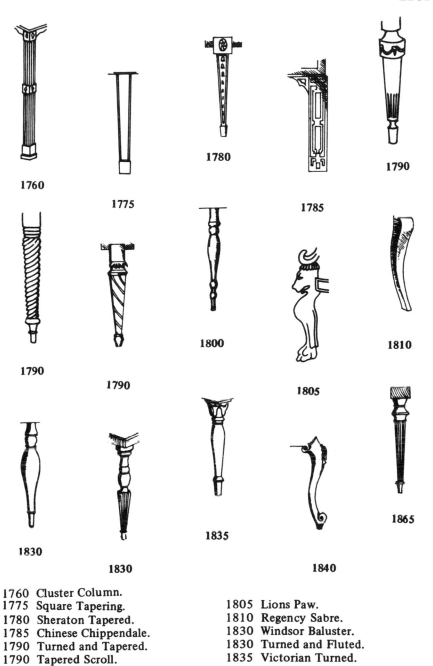

1760

1775

1780

1785

1790

1790

1790

1800

1805

1810

1830

1830

1835

1840

1865

1760 Cluster Column.
1775 Square Tapering.
1780 Sheraton Tapered.
1785 Chinese Chippendale.
1790 Turned and Tapered.
1790 Tapered Scroll.
1790 Tapered Spiral.
1800 Windsor Turned.

1805 Lions Paw.
1810 Regency Sabre.
1830 Windsor Baluster.
1830 Turned and Fluted.
1835 Victorian Turned.
1840 Victorian Cabriole.
1865 Victorian Reeded.

123

PEDIMENTS

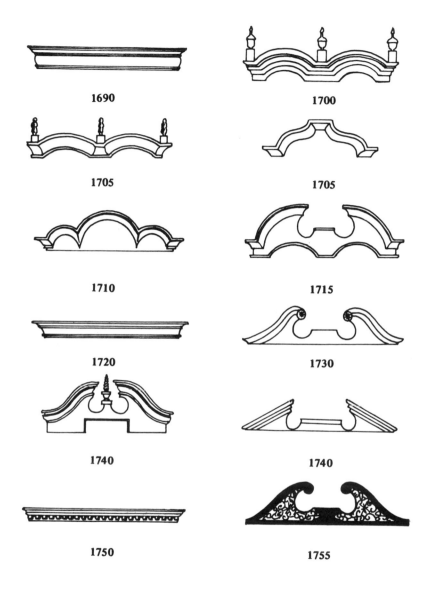

1690

1700

1705

1705

1710

1715

1720

1730

1740

1740

1750

1755

1690 Swell frieze.
1700 Queen Anne.
1705 Double arch.
1705 Queen Anne.
1710 Triple arch.
1715 Broken circular.

1720 Cavetto.
1730 Swan neck.
1740 Banner top.
1740 Broken arch.
1750 Dentil cornice.
1755 Fret cut.

INDEX

126